MW01473863

Andrew McCoy

To Ronnie

JOKES that STEM from a CHILD

A Family Joke Book

ANDREW MCCOY

Copyright © 2023 Andrew McCoy

All rights reserved. This book is copyright protected. It is only for personal use. No portion of this publication may be reproduced, distributed, or transmitted in any form or by any means, including photocopying, recording, or other electronic or mechanical methods, without the prior written permission of the publisher and author, except as permitted by U.S. copyright law. For information about permission to reproduce selections from this book, contact Andrew McCoy at sssberry@ yahoo.com.

Disclaimer Notice: Please note the information contained within this document is for educational and entertainment purposes only. All effort has been executed to present accurate, up to date, reliable, complete information. No warranties of any kind are declared or implied. Readers acknowledge that the author is not engaged in the rendering of legal financial, medical, or profession advice. The content within this book has been derived from various sources. Please consult a licensed professional before attempting any techniques outlined in this book.

By reading this document, the reader agrees that under no circumstances is the author responsible for any losses, direct or indirect, that are incurred as a result of the use of the information contained within this document, including, but not limited to, errors, omissions, or inaccuracies.

Book Cover by Andrew McCoy
Photos Credit by Andrew McCoy

ISBN 979-8-21849-158-1 (paperback)

Printed in the United States of America

For information about special discounts available for bulk purchases, sales promotions, fundraising and educational needs, contact Andrew McCoy at sssberry@yahoo.com

Published by Andrew McCoy

This book is dedicated to my supportive and loving family. My Mom helped me with writing and publishing the book. My brother Stevie shared his ideas and thoughts for many of my jokes. Finally, my Dad also shared with me topics for possible jokes.

This book is also dedicated to my special Nana because she always laughed at ALL of my jokes.

Contents

GENERAL JOKES

Q: What do you call someone struck by lightning?

A: Thunderstruck

Q: What do you call the bottom of a foggy sea?

A: Foggy bottoms

Q: What is a vacuum's personality?

A: It is a very sucky personality

Q: What do you call someone upside down?

A: Bottoms up

Q: What do people in jail listen to?

A: The jail house rock

Q: What do people call someone walking down a road that is on fire?

A: A Trailblazer

Q: What do you call a box with TNT?

A: A boom box

Q: What do people call an explosive band?

A: Dynamite

Q: What do you say when you see a person cooking while walking over a cliff?

A: A recipe for disaster

Q: What should you say when something hits your head?

A: Oops up side your head

Q: What does a frozen skeleton say?

A: I am chilled to the bone.

Q: What did the matches say to the wood?

A: We have got you out matched.

Q: What does the captain of a cruise ship about to crash say?

A: We are cruising for a bruising.

Q: What does a skeleton say when a person gets him mad?

A: I have a bone to pick with you.

Q: What do you call a person getting slapped by a stick?

A: Slap- stick- comedy

Q: What did the rock say to the concert goers?

A: I will rock your world.

Q: What do you call a guilty pipe?

A: A faulty pipe

Q: What do you call a rock that fights a sock?

A: Rock'em sock'em

Q: What do you say when you rip a piece of paper?

A: Let it rip

Q: What do you call an annoying person?

A: A bratwurst

Q: What does a straw say to water?

A: Suck it up

Q: What does a 2D shape say to a 3D shape?

A: Look at my good side

Q: What do you call a person who gets hit by a golf ball?

A: A hole in one

Q: What do you call a town of people mowing their lawn?

A: Motown

Q: What did the hurricane say to the surfer?

A: See you Monsoon

Q: What did Saturday say to Sunday?

A: Ha! I come before you.

Q: What do you call people riding in a car who are happy?

A: A joy ride

Q: What is a fire caught in a cross?

A: A cross fire.

Q: What did the astronaut say to his friend?

A: Houston, we got a problem.

Q: What do you call a duke who makes a mess?

A: The Duke of Making a Mess

Q: What is a person who gets pushed over?

A: A *push* over

Q: What do you get when you mix a runner and a camera?

A: A dashcam

SCIENTIFIC JOKES

Q: What do you call a guy that dances to the radio?

A: Radioactive

Q: What did oxygen say to nitrogen?

A: You are so cool.

Q: What do you call a flower that shoots out pollen?

A: Flower power

Q: What music do the electrons in an atom listen to?

A: The atomic boogie

Q: What do you call radioactive waste?

A: A hot mess

Q: What did the sand say to the seaweed?

A: You are all washed up.

Q: What do you call a star's currency?

A: A star bill

Q: What does water like to eat?

A: Salt

Q: What do people call nobodies?

A: Antibodies

Q: What did oxygen say to hydrogen?

A: You have an explosive personality.

Q: What did the balloon say to helium?

A: You lift me off my feet.

OUTSIDE-THE-BOX JOKES

Q: What do you call a person whose head is made of nuts?

A: A nut head

Q: What do you call a nut that has a brief case?

A: A nut case

Q: What do you call a crack in Antarctica?

A: Cold cuts

Q: What does someone say when they eat too much?

A: Fed up

Q: Where does stale bread go to?

A: The national stale bread committee

Q: What do you call someone who snickers?

A: Mr. Snickers

Q: What does a frozen skeleton say?

A: I am chilled to the bone.

Q: What did the nut say to the bolt?

A: You are screwed up.

Q: What did the cornstalks say to the farmer with the sickle?

A: You are farmed and dangerous.

Q: What did the person say to the nosy rope?

A: Do not get so wrapped up in people's business.

Q: Who did the Snowflake marry?

A: Snow White

Q: What kind of suit does a lawyer wear?

A: A law suit

Q: What do you call the girl who always walks to the left?

A: Lefty Lucy

Q: What do you call a person who cleans his room?

A: Righty-tidy

Q: What do you call cash in ice?

A: Cold hard cash

Q: What do you call a terminal that is destroyed?

A: Terminated

Q: What does a tornado say when it wins in football?

A: Touchdown

Q: What does a baker drink when he is baking?

A: Baking soda

Q: What stakes do vampires dislike?

A: A Sunday Porterhouse

Q: What do you call a toy doing yoga?

A: Toyoga

MATH JOKES

Q: What do you call the place between 50 and 52?

A: Area 51

Q: What do you say to 21?

A: Drop and give me twenty

Q: What do you call negative three?

A: Three below

Q: What did people on rank 4 say to people on rank 2?

A: We out rank you.

Q: What dance does a rectangle do?

A: The rectango

Q: What dance does a square like to do?

A: The square dance

Q: What did the glue say to the hard-working math student?

A: Stick to it

Q: What did the square say to the camera man?

A: Get my good side

ANIMAL JOKES

Q: What do you say to a lobster caught stealing?

A: You have been caught red handed.

Q: What do you call a lobster that turns around?

A: A lobster roll

Q: What do you call a stinky chicken?

A: A funky chicken

Q: What do you say when a chicken walks in front of you?

A: Hello breakfast!

Q: What do you say to a dumb ox?

A: You are an oxymoron.

Q: What does someone call a worm in a library?

A: A Book worm

Q: What is an earthworm's personality?

A: They are very earthy.

Q: Who do you call to get rid of bugs?

A: The swat team

Q: What do you call a kangaroo with money?

A: Buck-a-Roo

Q: What do you call a weird female deer?

A: A weirdo

Q: What is so bad about a skunk's smell?

A: It is bad because its smell reeked havoc.

Q: What do you say to a pig?

A: Hello breakfast!

FOOD JOKES

Q: What are peas put into?

A: Pecans

Q: What did the apple say to the sad banana?

A: Ripen up

Q: What do you call a cookie that laughs?

A: Snickerdoodle

Q: What is a grouch that ate lemons?

A: A sour grouch

Q: What does the strawberry say to the blueberry?

A: Stop being blue and become happy

Q: What do you call a strawberry that laughs?

A: Chuckle berry

Q: What do you call the greatest ice of all time?

A: Ice Supreme

Q: What is a dumb peanut?

A: A dumb nut

Q: What do you call a vegetable saying slang words?

A: A fresh vegetable

Q: What does a salad want for a dress?

A: Salad dressing

Q: What do you call eggs that are stolen?

A: Poached eggs

Q: What do you call people who lift up flaps?

A: Flapjacks

ABOUT THE AUTHOR

Andrew is a fifteen year old boy who loves to tell jokes that he creates to his family members. He is talented at creating his own jokes, and this encouraged him to write his own joke book when he was eleven years old. If many of his family members laughed at the joke, then he would add it to his joke book. He is also interested in science, math, space, and especially rockets. He enjoys reading and learning about NASA, rockets, and the planets. He has a younger brother who is also writing his own book about cooking.